Title	Piano/Vocal	Guitar

INTEGRITY

MUSIC®

EXCLUSIVELY DISTRIBUTED BY

HAL•LEONARD®
CORPORATION

7777 W. BLUEMOUND RD. P.O. BOX 13819 MILWAUKEE, WI 53213

Come In From The Outside

Words and Music by
ISRAEL HOUGHTON and
MELEASA HOUGHTON

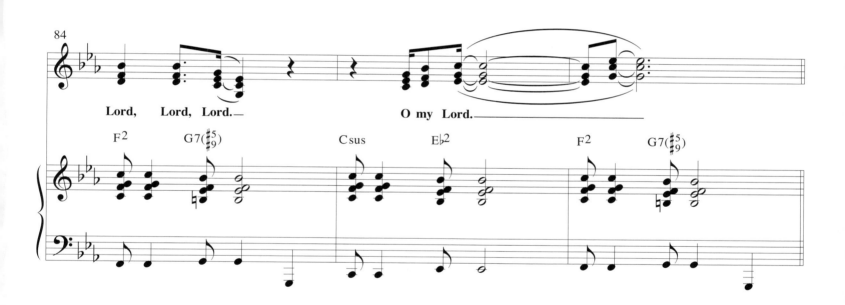

Again I Say Rejoice

Words and Music by
ISRAEL HOUGHTON and
AARON LINDSEY

Come bless___ the Lord. Come bless___ the Lord.

Draw near___ to wor - ship Christ,___ the Lord and bless___ His name,

His ho - ly name, de - clar - ing He___ is good.___

Again I Say Rejoice (Reprise)

Words and Music by
ISRAEL HOUGHTON and
AARON LINDSEY

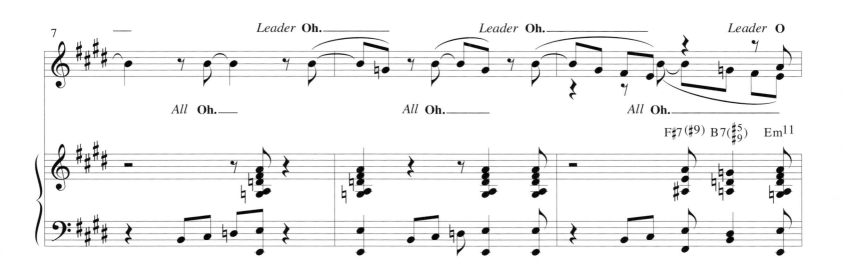

26

We Win

**Words and Music by
ISRAEL HOUGHTON and
AARON LINDSEY**

We got the vic-to-ry. Oh,

we got the vic-to-ry. It's all be-cause of You we win.

All Around

**Words and Music by
CURT COFFIELD, ISRAEL HOUGHTON
and AARON LINDSEY**

40

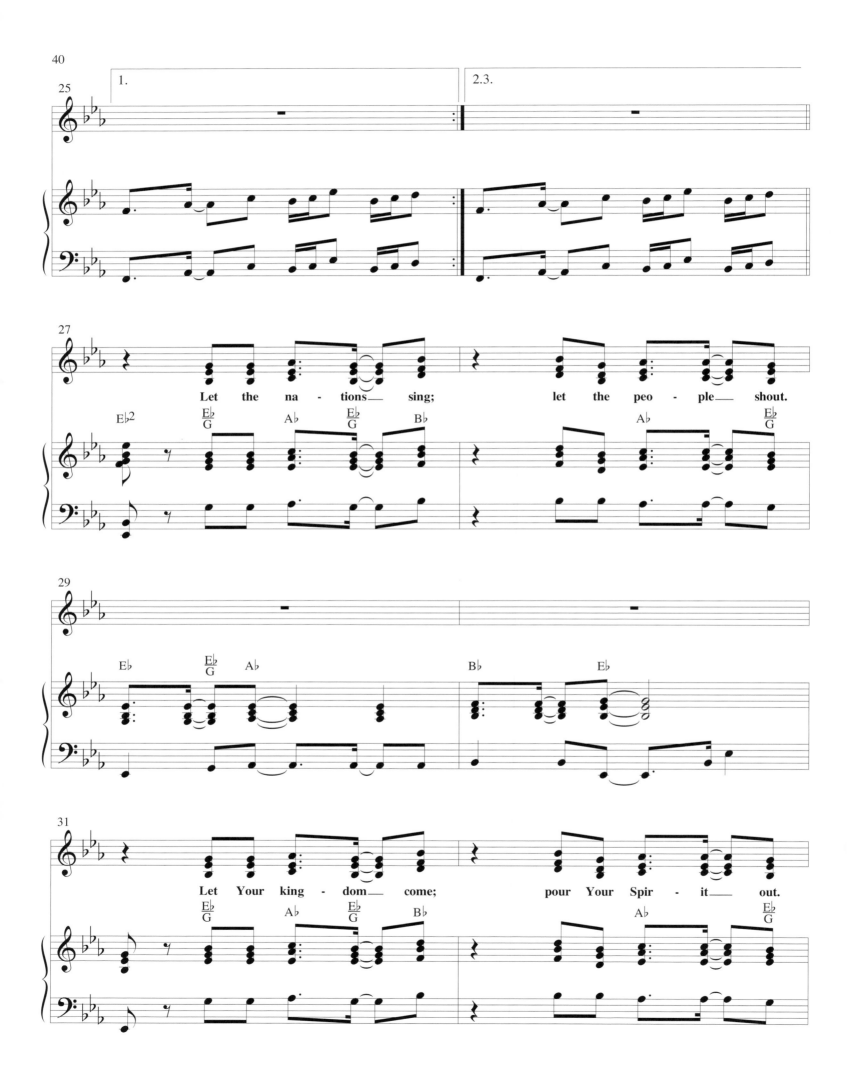

42

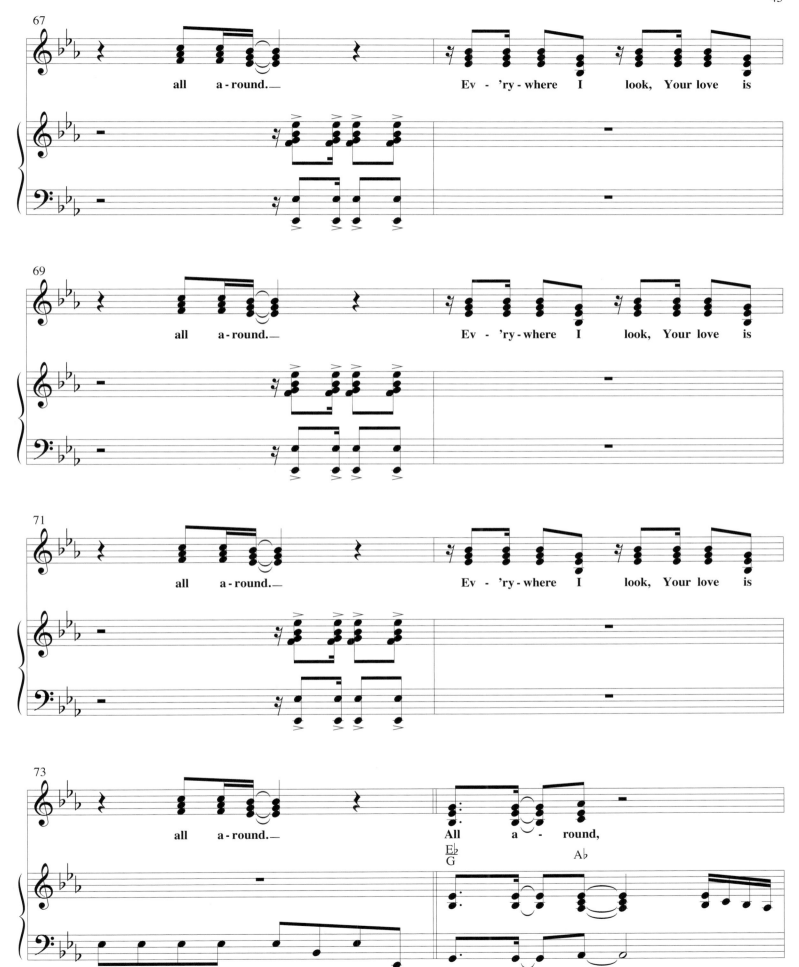

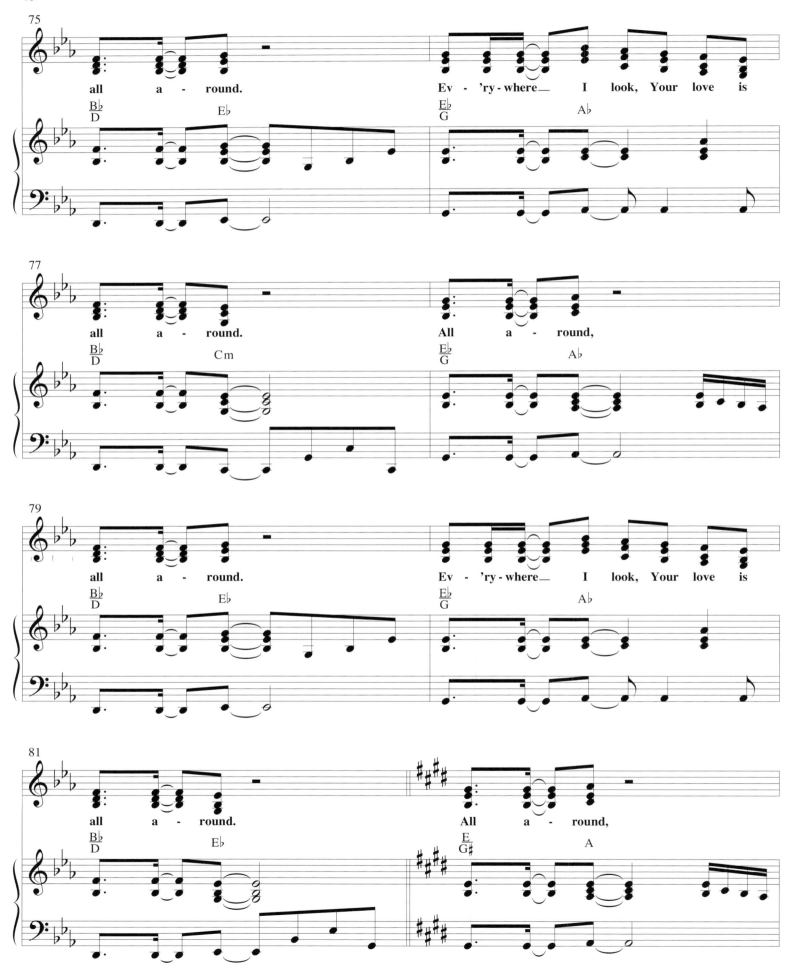

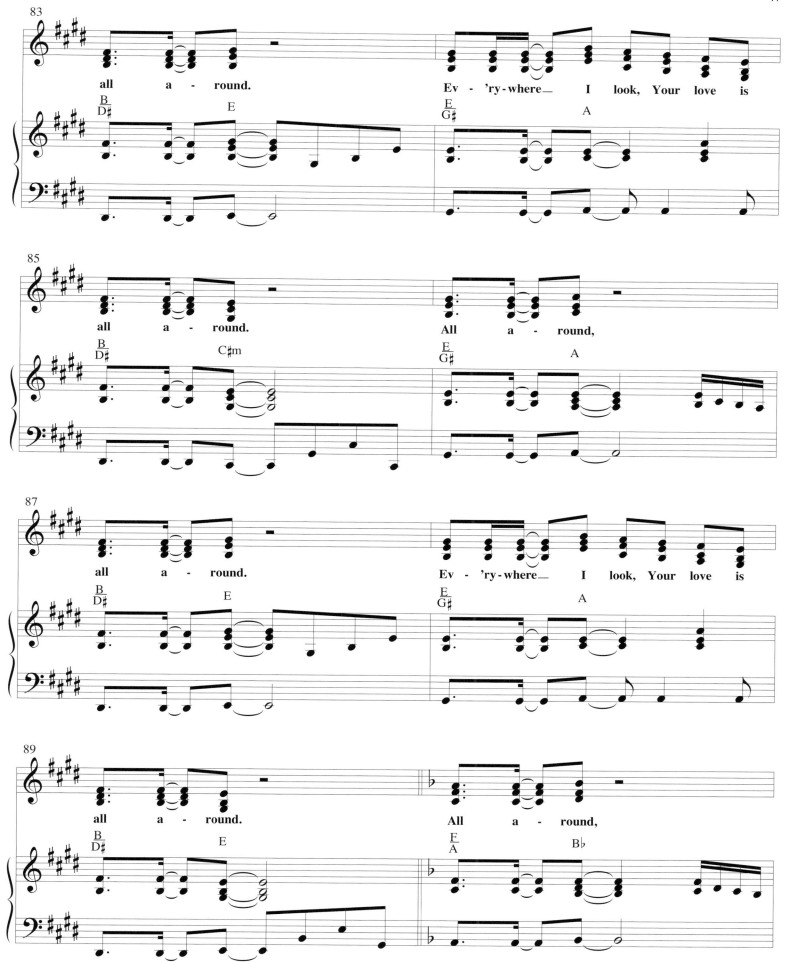

You've Made Me Glad/Who Is Like The Lord?

**Words and Music by
ISRAEL HOUGHTON, AARON LINDSEY
and CINDY CRUSE RATCLIFF**

54

I Hear The Sound

Words and Music by
ISRAEL HOUGHTON

So Easy To Love/Friend Of God

Words and Music by
DONALD CLAY

ea - sy to love You, You're my ___ Friend. ___

FRIEND OF GOD (Words and Music by Michael Grungor and Israel Houghton)

I am a friend___ of God.___

I am a friend___ of God.___

I am a friend___ of God.___

___ He calls___ me friend.___

Friend Of God

**Words and Music by
MICHAEL GUNGOR and
ISRAEL HOUGHTON**

He calls—— me friend.————

What—— a—— priv - i - lege it is,———— yeah!————

Who am I—— that You—— are mind - ful—— of—— me,——

that—— You—— hear—— me———— when—— I call?——

called me friend.

I am a friend of God,

I am a friend of God,

I am a friend of God, You call me friend.

3rd time: drums only
5th time: Instrumental

Friend

Words and Music by
ISRAEL HOUGHTON, MELEASA HOUGHTON,
AARON LINDSEY and KEVIN SINGLETON

1st time: Worship Leader (with freedom)
2nd time: All (Men 8vb)

Friend Medley:

Joy Of My Desire *with* **No, Not One,**
What A Friend We Have In Jesus *and* **Friend**

Words and Music by
JENNIFER RANDOLPH

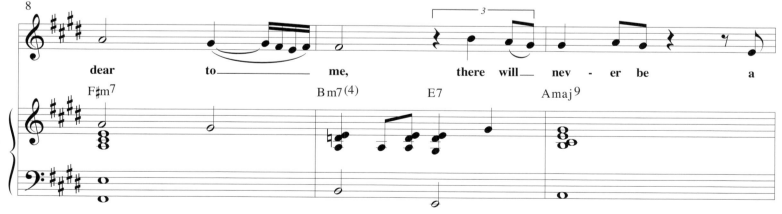

NO, NOT ONE (Words: Johnson Oatman, Jr./Music: George C. Hugg) Traditional - Public Domain

WHAT A FRIEND WE HAVE IN JESUS *(Words: Joseph M. Scriven/Music: Charles C. Converse) Traditional - Public Domain*

FRIEND (Israel Houghton, Meleasa Houghton, Aaron Lindsey and Kevin Singleton)

Rise Within Us

*with **Another Breakthrough***

**Words and Music by
ISRAEL HOUGHTON
and AARON LINDSEY**

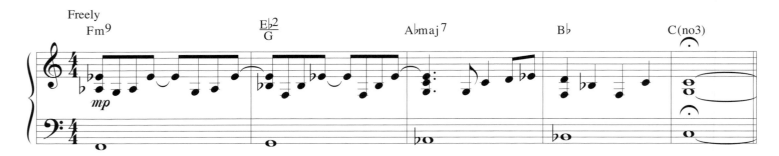

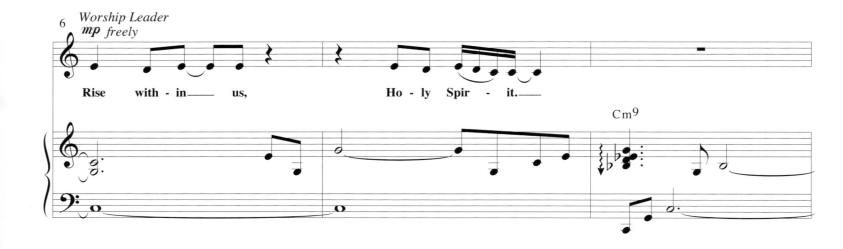

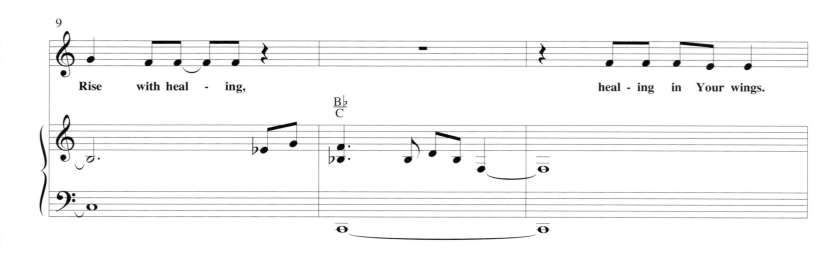

ANOTHER BREAKTHROUGH (Israel Houghton and Aaron Lindsey)

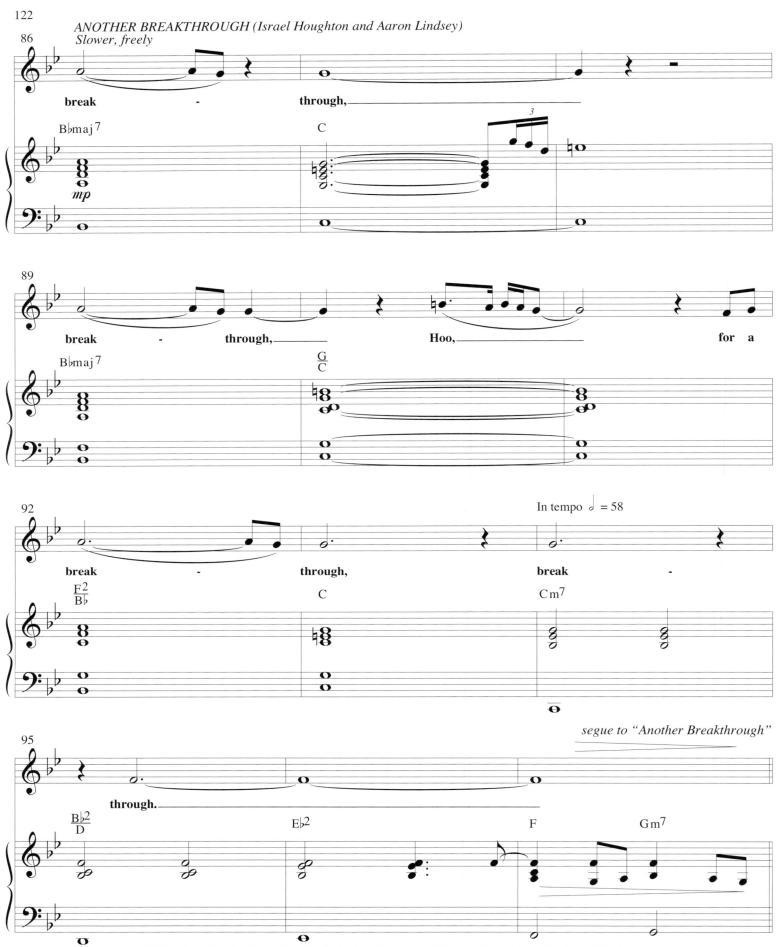

Another Breakthrough

Words and Music by
ISRAEL HOUGHTON
and AARON LINDSEY

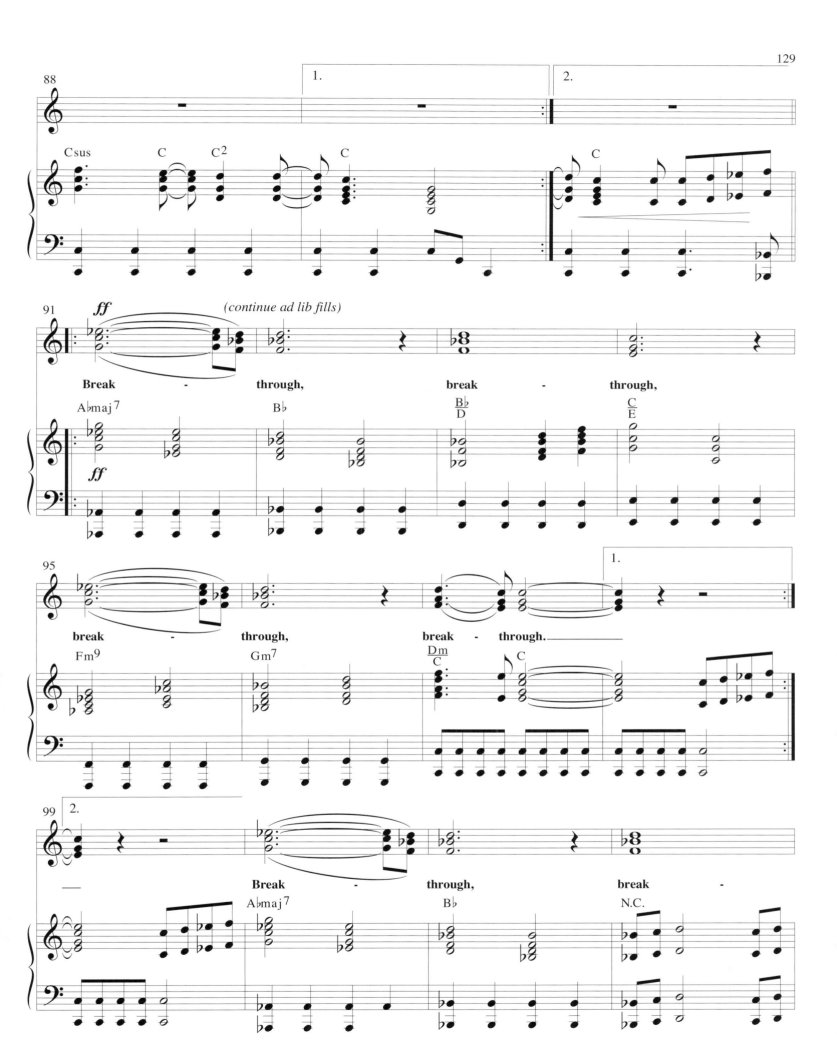

Lord Of The Breakthrough

Words and Music by
ISRAEL HOUGHTON
and AARON LINDSEY

Breathe Into Me

Words and Music by
ISRAEL HOUGHTON

Awesome Medley: I Stand In Awe (Maravillado Estoy)

with **Awesome In This Place**

**Words and Music by
MARK ALTROGGE**

AWESOME IN THIS PLACE (David Billington)
Worship Leader

wor - thy of___ all praise.___ To You, our lives___ we raise.___ You are

awe - some in___ this place,___ might - y___ God.___

(ad lib fills)

segue to "Medley: Here I Am To Worship"

Here I Am To Worship

with **You Are Good**

Words and Music by
TIM HUGHES

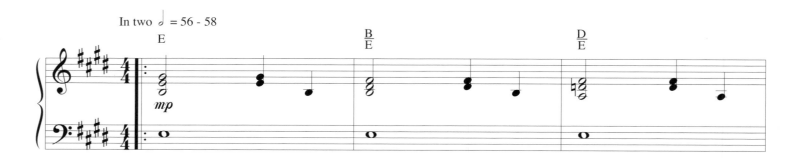

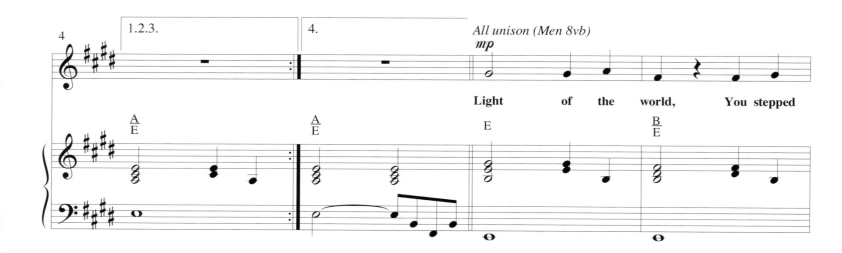

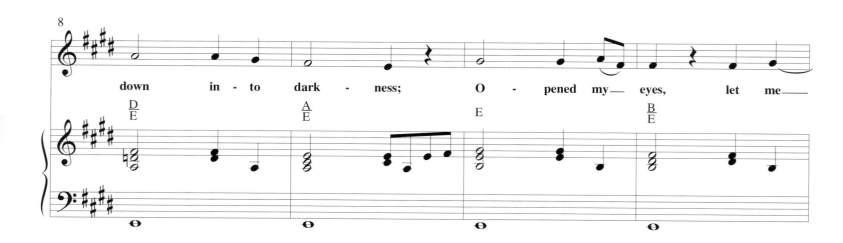

162

Holy

Words and Music by
**ISRAEL HOUGHTON, MELEASA HOUGHTON
and AARON LINDSEY**

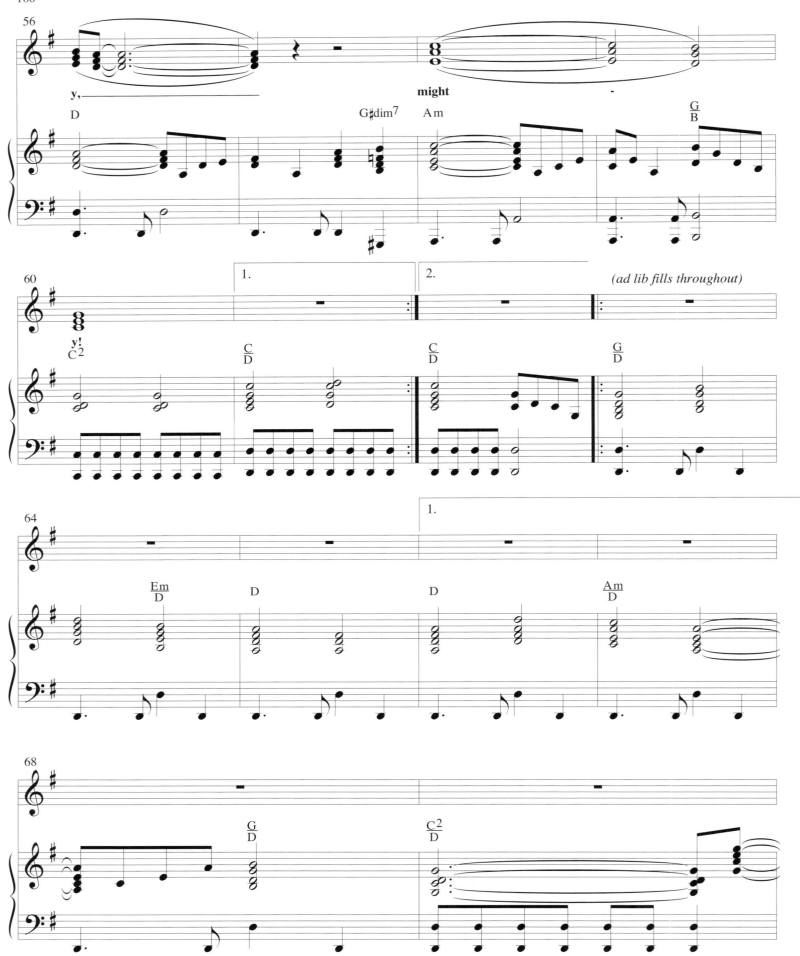

Going To Another Level

**Words and Music by
ISRAEL HOUGHTON
and AARON LINDSEY**

Come In From The Outside

Israel Houghton and Meleasa Houghton

INTRO
| Csus | B♭6 | A♭maj7 | Gm7 | Fm9 | Gm7 *(repeat)* | | |
| Csus | B♭6 | A♭maj7 | Gm7 | Fm9 | Gm7 | Csus | B♭6 | A♭maj7/D | Gm7 | Gm7/F |

VERSE
N.C.
Come in from the outside; don't be ashamed. Come in from the outside and bless His name, now.
                                        A♭maj9   G7(♯5♯9)
It's all on the inside where His glory reigns.   Enter in. Enter in.
N.C.
Come in from the outside just as you are. Come in from the outside; you're not too far, no.
           E♭maj9   Fm9   Gm7   A♭maj9   G7(♯5♯9)
It's all on the inside.   Simply open your heart.   Enter in. Enter in.

CHORUS
Csus   E♭2   F2   G7(♯5♯9)   Csus   E♭2   F2   G7(♯5♯9)   Csus   E♭2
Everybody, everybody.   Everybody, everybody.   Everybody, everybody.
F2   G7(♯5♯9)   C2/E   Fm9   G7(♯5♯9)   Csus
   Let everything that has breath praise the Lord. Everybody, everybody   praise.

B♭6/C   A♭maj7/C   Gm7/C   A♭maj7/C   Gm7/C   Csus   B♭6/D   Fm9   Gm7   A♭   B♭

(repeat Verse and Chorus)

BRIDGE
Cm7   Cm11
We're the generation that will give You praise and adoration.
                                     Edim7   Fm7   Gm7   F/A   G7(♯5♯9)
Let Your kingdom come; let Your will be done. Establish   now Your throne, O my Lord.
(repeat several times)

Csus E♭2   F2   G7(♯5♯9)   Csus E♭2   F2   G7(♯5♯9)
   O my Lord, Lord, Lord, Lord.   O my Lord, Lord, Lord, Lord.
Csus E♭2   F2   G7(♯5♯9)   Csus E♭2   F2   G7(♯5♯9)
   Praise You, Lord, Lord, Lord, Lord.   Praise You, Lord, Lord, Lord, Lord.
Csus E♭2   F2   G7(♯5♯9)   Csus E♭2   F2   G7(♯5♯9)
   Love You, Lord, Lord, Lord, Lord.   O my Lord.

(repeat Chorus twice)

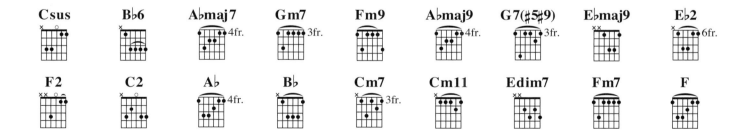

Csus   B♭6   A♭maj7   Gm7   Fm9   A♭maj9   G7(♯5♯9)   E♭maj9   E♭2

F2   C2   A♭   B♭   Cm7   Cm11   Edim7   Fm7   F

Again I Say Rejoice

Israel Houghton and Aaron Lindsey

CHORUS

E   A2/C♯ C♯m7   Cmaj7   D
Rejoice in the Lord al-   ways, and again I say, and again I say.
E   A2/C♯ C♯m7   Cmaj7   D   E
Rejoice in the Lord al-   ways, and again I say, and again I say rejoice.

VERSE

E   D   A2/C♯   E
Come bless the Lord. Come bless the Lord. Draw near to worship Christ, the Lord
                                   D   A2/C♯ E
And bless His name, His holy name, declaring He is good.
(repeat)

PRE-CHORUS

Am7   Bm7   Cmaj7   D
O that men would praise Him. O that men would praise Him.

(repeat Chorus)
(repeat Verse)
(repeat Pre-Chorus)
(repeat Chorus twice)

BRIDGE

Em11
O that men would praise His name, praise His name to the ends of the earth.
                                               C/D Em11
O that men would praise His name, praise His name to the ends of the earth.
                                  F♯7sus E7sus   D7sus   Bm7
O that men would praise His name, praise His name to   the   ends of the uh, earth.
Em11   Am9   Bm9
O that men would praise His name. Again I say, again I say.
(repeat)
 Cmaj9   Dmaj7   Am9   Bm9
Again I say, again I say. Again I say, again I say.

(repeat Chorus twice)

TAG

B/C♯ C♯m7 G/C Am/C G/C D E B/C♯ C♯m7 G/C Am/C G/C D
                               Rejoice.

E F♯m/C♯ C♯m7 Cmaj7   D E/G♯ Esus/F♯ E B♯dim7 C♯m7 F♯m7 Cmaj7 D Esus E
Rejoice.   Rejoice.   Rejoice.   Rejoice.   Re-   joice.

E   A2   C♯m7   Cmaj7   D   Am7   Bm7   Em11

C   F♯7sus   E7sus   D7sus   Am9   Bm9   Cmaj9   Dmaj7

B   G   Am   F♯m   Esus   B♯dim7   F♯m7

Again I Say Rejoice (Reprise)

Israel Houghton and Aaron Lindsey

INTRO
Em11   **F#7(#9)   B7(#5#9)**
Oh. Oh. Oh. Oh. Oh. Oh. Oh. Oh.
Em11
O that men would praise Him. O that men would praise Him.

O that men would praise Him. O that men would praise Him.

Let the nations praise Him. Let the nations praise Him.
                                        F#7(#9)   B7(#5#9)
Let the nations praise Him. Let the nations praise   Him.

BRIDGE
Em11
O that men would praise His name, praise His name to the ends of the earth.
                                                        F#7(#9)   B7(#5#9)
O that men would praise His name, praise His name to the ends of the earth.
Em11   **F#7sus   E7sus   D7sus   Bm7**
O that men would praise His name, praise His name to   the   ends of the uh, earth.
Em11   **Am9   Bm9   Cmaj9   Dmaj7   Am9   Bm9**
O that men would praise His name. Again I say, again I say. Again I say, again I say. Again I say, again I say.

CHORUS
N.C.
Rejoice in the Lord always, and again I say, and again I say.
                            Cmaj7   Dmaj7
Rejoice in the Lord always, and again I say, again I say.
E   **F#m/C#   C#m7   Cmaj7   D**
Rejoice in the Lord al-   ways, and again I say, again I say.
E   **A2/C#   C#m7   Cmaj7   D**   **F#m/C#   C#m7**
Rejoice in the Lord al-   ways, and again I say, again I say rejoice.

TAG
Cmaj7   D   **E/G#   Esus/F#   E   B#dim7   C#m7   F#m7**
Rejoice.   Rejoice.
Cmaj7   D   Esus   E
Rejoice.   Re-   joice.

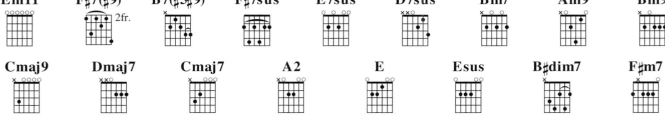

We Win

Israel Houghton and Aaron Lindsey

INTRO
| G♭maj9 | Fm7 | E♭m11 | Fm7 | G♭maj9 | Fm7 | E♭m11 | Fm7 | G♭maj9 |

Oh,   oh,   oh,   oh.

| Fm7 | E♭m11 | Fm7 | G♭maj9 | B♭6 | A♭maj7/B♭ |

Oh,   oh,   we   win.

VERSE
G♭maj9   Fm7   E♭m7   Fm7   G♭maj9   Fm7   E♭m7   Fm7
We overcome by Your Word.   Your Word will always prevail.
G♭maj9   Fm7   E♭m7   A♭m7   A♭m7/D♭   G♭maj9   A♭maj9/B♭
We overcome by the blood of the Lamb and the promise we have in   You.
G♭maj9   Fm7   E♭m7   Fm7   G♭maj9   Fm7   E♭m7   Fm7
We lift our voice with a shout.   You always cause us to   triumph.
G♭maj9   Fm7   E♭m7   E♭m/C   F7(♯9)   A♭maj9/B♭
We lift our hands like it's already done, for it's already   won   by You.

CHORUS
G♭maj9   Fm7   E♭m11   Fm7   G♭maj9   A♭   B♭m7
We win because of   You. We over- come and conquer in Your name.
G♭maj9   Fm7   E♭m11   F7(♯9)   B♭m7   E♭9(♯11)   A♭m9   D♭13
We win because of   You; all things are   pos-   sible.   We win.

(repeat Intro and Verse)
(repeat Chorus twice)

BRIDGE *(1st time Instrumental)*
B♭m9   G7(♯5♯9)   E♭9   C7(♭5)   F7(♯9)
Oh,   we got the victory. We got the victory.
B♭m9   G7(♯5♯9)   E♭9   C7(♭5)   F7(♯9)
Oh,   we got the victory. It's all because of You we win.
(repeat four times; third repeat Instrumental)
(repeat Chorus)

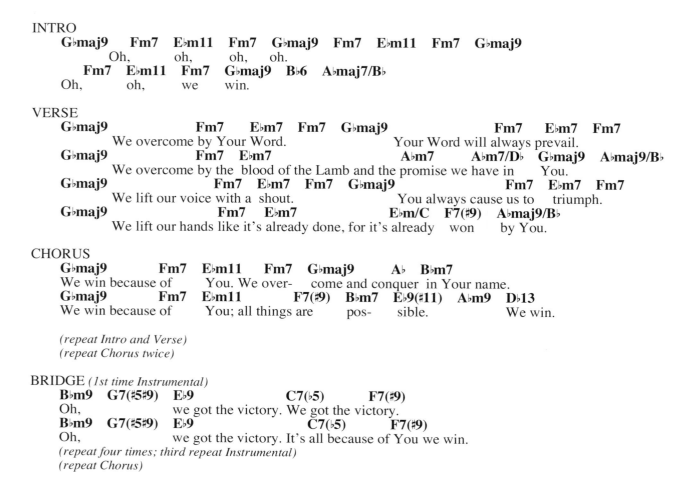

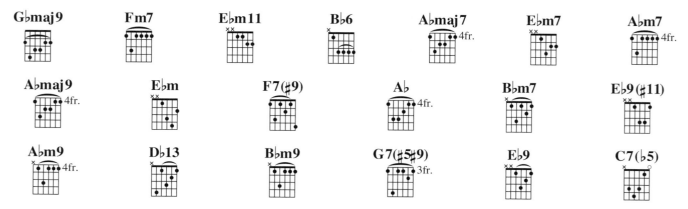

All Around (page 1 of 2)

Curt Coffield, Israel Houghton and Aaron Lindsey

INTRO
E♭2   A♭2   B♭/D   E♭2   A♭2   B♭/D *(repeat)*

CHORUS
E♭   A♭   B♭   E♭   A♭   B♭   E♭ (Cm *on repeats***)**
All around, all around. Everywhere I look, Your love is all around.
E♭   A♭   B♭   E♭   A♭   B♭   E♭
All around, all around. Everywhere I look, Your love is all around.
(repeat twice)

VERSE
E♭2   E♭/G   A♭   E♭/G   B♭   A♭   E♭/G   E♭   E♭/G   A♭   B♭   E♭
      Let the na- tions   sing; let the people shout.
E♭/G   A♭   E♭/G   B♭   A♭   E♭/G   E♭   E♭/G   A♭   B♭   E♭   Fm/D   G7(♯5)
Let Your kingdom   come; pour Your Spirit out.
B♭/C   Cm7   B♭/D   E♭   E♭sus   E♭   E♭2/G   B♭/C   Cm7   B♭/A♭   E♭/A♭   Fm7   A♭/B♭
Mani- fest,   manifest Your love.   Mani- fest, mani- fest Your love,

(repeat Chorus)
(repeat Verse)
(repeat Chorus)

BRIDGE 1
A♭   E♭   A♭/E♭   E♭   Bdim7
   Your love is too deep to navigate   and it's too   high to climb.
Cm   G/B   Cm   B♭/D   Cm/E♭   E♭/F   F13   E♭m/A♭   D♭/A♭   A♭m7   Fm7/B♭
   But still it's a-   vaila- ble   time after time after time   after   time after time.
**   A7(♭5)   A♭maj7   A♭/B♭   B♭   A♭/B♭   Fm/B♭   E♭2**
Your love   lifted me. It's too deep to nav- i- gate;   it's too high to climb, oh.
G7(♯5♯9)   Cm11   B♭/D   Cm/E♭   B♭/D   Cm/E♭   Edim7   E♭/F   A♭m7   Fm7/B♭
Oh, but   still, still it's avail- a- ble   time after time after time after time after time.

Can I get a witness?

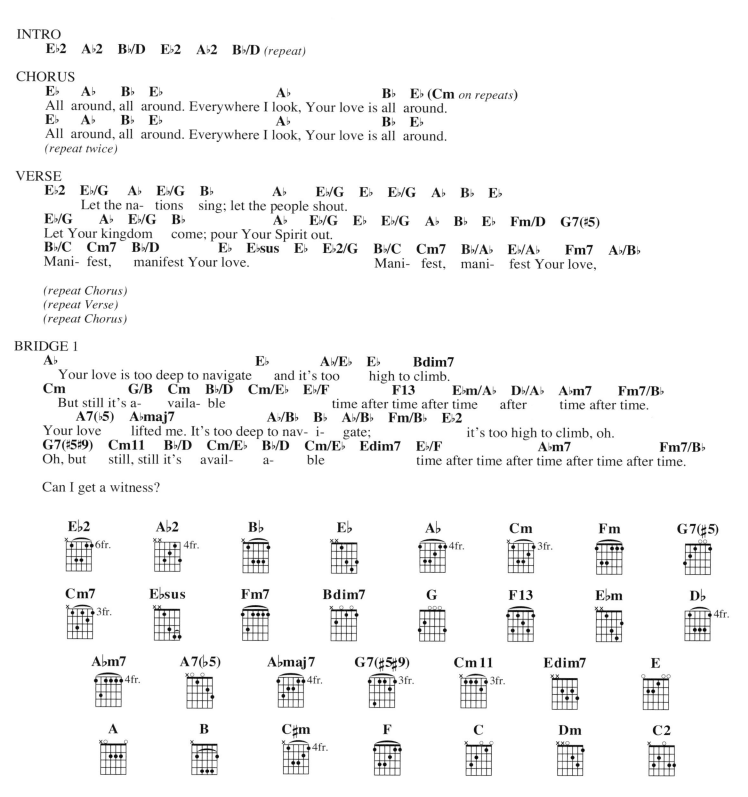

All Around (page 2 of 2)

BRIDGE 2
N.C.
Hey, now. Oh, now. Oh, now. Oh, now.

Hey, now. Oh, now. Oh, now. Oh, now.
E♭2
Everywhere I look, Your love is all around. Everywhere I look, Your love is all around.

Everywhere I look, Your love is all around. Everywhere I look, Your love is all around.

Everywhere I look, Your love is all around. Everywhere I look, Your love is all around.

(repeat Chorus)

CHORUS *(in E)*
    E/G♯ **A**   **B/D♯** **E**   **E/G♯**   **A**   **B/D♯** **C♯m**
    All   around, all   around. Everywhere I look, Your love is all   around.
    E/G♯ **A**   **B/D♯** **E**   **E/G♯**   **A**   **B/D♯** **E**
    All   around, all   around. Everywhere I look, Your love is all   around.

CHORUS *(in F)*
    F/A **B♭**   **C/E** **F**   **F/A**   **B♭**   **C/E** **Dm**
    All   around, all   around. Everywhere I look, Your love is all   around.
    F/A **B♭**   **C/E** **F**   **F/A**   **B♭**   **C/E** **F**
    All   around, all   around. Everywhere I look, Your love is all   around.
    F/A   **B♭**   **C/E** **F**   **F/A**   **B♭**   **C/E** **F**
    Everywhere I look, Your love is all   around. Everywhere I look, Your love is all   around.
    F/A   **B♭**   **C2** **E♭2** **C/E** **F**
    Everywhere I look, Your love is all around. All   around.

You've Made Me Glad/Who Is Like The Lord? (page 1 of 2)

Israel Houghton, Aaron Lindsey and Cindy Cruse Ratcliff

INTRO
A♭maj9   Gm7 Fm7 Gm7   A♭maj9   Gm7   Fm7   A7(♯9)   A♭maj9
    Oh, oh,   oh, oh,   oh, oh,   I will say that the Lord, He has made me glad.
Gm7 Fm7   Gm7 A♭maj9   Gm7 Fm7 A9(♯5)
Oh, oh,   yeah, yeah,   oh, oh.

VERSE
           A♭maj9   Gm7 Fm7   Gm7 A♭maj9
You put a song in my heart,   rhythm in my step,
           Gm7 Fm7   A7(♯5)
Praise as my garment   for the spirit of heaviness, yeah, yeah,
A♭maj9   Gm7 Fm7   Gm7 A♭maj9   Gm7 Fm7
Beauty for ashes,   joy for my pain.   Love overwhelming   causes me to say

CHORUS
Cm   B♭/C Cm   Fm   G7(♯5)
  You've made me glad.   You've made me glad.
Cm   B♭/C Cm   Fm   E♭6 Fm/D   Gaug Cm
  You've made me glad. Lord, I will re-   joice because You   have.
     B♭/C Cm   Fm   G7(♯5)
You've made me glad.   You've made me glad.
Cm   B♭/C Cm   Fm   Cm/E♭ B♭/D   A7(♭5) A♭maj9 Gm7 Fm7
  You've made me glad. Lord, I will re-   joice because You   have   made me glad.
Gm7 A♭maj9   Gm7 Fm7 A9(♯5)
Oh,   yeah.

(repeat Verse and Chorus)

TRANSITION
Fm7   A9(♯5)   Gm7 Fm7   Gm7 A♭maj7
Lord, I will rejoice because You have made   me glad.
  B7(♯9) Cm11 D7(♯9) G7(♯5) G7   Cm
  I will   rejoice;   You   have   made me glad.

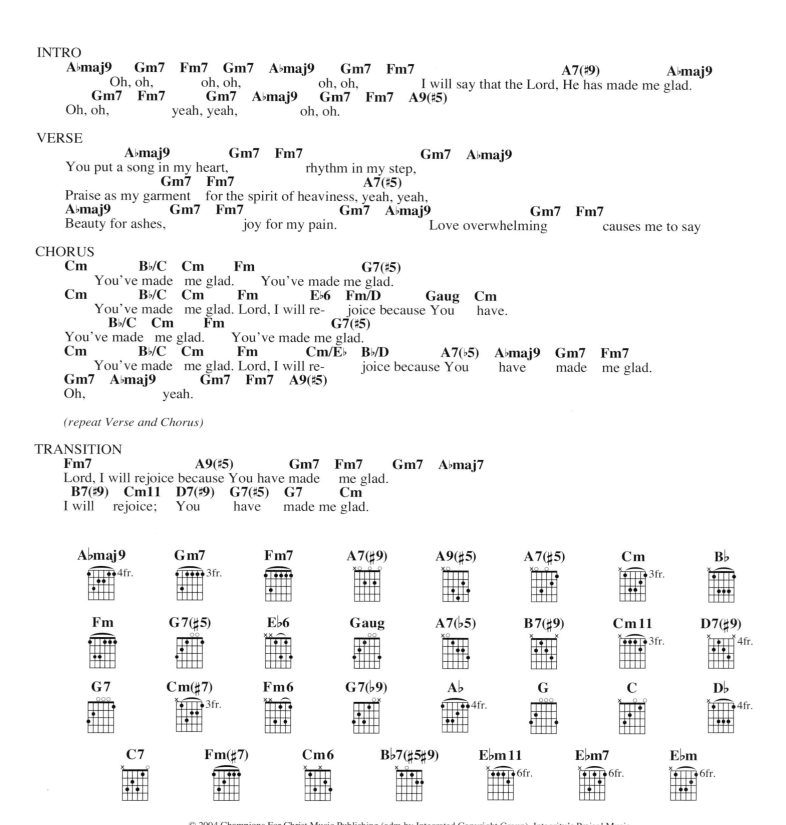

You've Made Me Glad/Who Is Like The Lord? (page 2 of 2)

BRIDGE 1 (1st time Instrumental)
```
       Cm        Cm(#7)  Cm7  Cm(#7)
So I will lift my hands and lift my voice.
       Fm6      G7(b9)            Cm     Cm(#7)  Cm7  Cm(#7)  Fm6  G7(b9)
The way I feel, I have no choice. You made me glad.
       Cm        Cm(#7)  Cm7   Cm(#7)  Fm6
I'm gonna dance and sing and  shout for joy and   praise Your name;
 G7(b9)          Cm     Cm(#7)  Cm7  Cm(#7)  Fm6  G7(b9)
I will rejoice. You made me glad.
```
(repeat twice)

BRIDGE 2
```
   Ab/G  G      Ab/G  G  Ab/G  G        Ab/G  Cm
You've made me glad.      You've made me glad.
   Ab/C  Cm     Ab/C  Cm  Ab/C  Cm  Ab/C      G
You've made me glad.   Lord, I will  rejoice because You have.
   Ab/G  G      Ab/G  G  Ab/G  G        Ab/G  Cm
You've made me glad.      You've made me glad.
   Ab/C  Cm     Ab/C  Cm     Ab/C                C  Db/C  C  Db/C  C7/E
You've made me glad.     Lord, I will rejoice because You         have.
     Fm/D  C  Fm  Fm(#7)  Fm7  Fm(#7)     Fm/D             G
Oh,       oh,           yeah. Na, na, na, na, na, na, na, na, na, na, na.
```

(repeat Chorus twice)

```
N.C.                  G7          Cm6
I will rejoice 'cause You have made me glad.
```

REPRISE
(repeat Bridge 1 twice)

BRIDGE 1 (in Eb minor)
```
 Bb7(#5#9)        Ebm11
      So I will lift my hands and lift my voice.

The way I feel, I have no choice. You made me glad.
 Bb7(#5#9)        Ebm11
      I'm gonna dance and sing and  shout for joy and praise Your name;
                        Bb7(#5#9)
I will rejoice. You made me glad.
```

WHO IS LIKE THE LORD *(Israel Houghton)*
CHORUS
```
 Ebm7                                                    Ebm     Fm/Ab
Lord, we declare. Who can compare? Who would even dare? 'Cause there is no one like You.
```
(repeat three times)
(optional segue into "I Hear The Sound")

I Hear The Sound (page 1 of 2)

Israel Houghton

INTRO
E♭m7   E♭m/G♭   Fm/A♭

VERSE
E♭m D♭/E♭ E♭m   E♭m7 A♭/E♭ E♭m7   D♭/E♭ E♭m D♭/E♭ E♭m   E♭m/G♭   Fm/A♭
I hear the   sound of a new breed   marching   toward the   gates of the enemy.
E♭m D♭/E♭ E♭m   E♭m7 A♭/E♭ E♭m7   D♭/E♭ E♭m D♭/E♭ E♭m   E♭m/G♭   Fm/A♭
I hear the   sound of a new breed   marching   toward the   gates of the enemy.
(repeat)
(Eight bar Instrumental/Spoken Section - no chord)
(repeat Verse)
(Sixteen bar Instrumental/Spoken Section)
(repeat Verse)
(Four bar Instrumental/Spoken Section)

ANTIPHONAL *(Congregation repeats after Worship Leader)*
N.C.   E♭m7   A♭/E♭ E♭m
So we're armed and dangerous, strong and serious, clothed in righteousness. It's a new breed.

Said a new breed, a new breed. We're talkin' 'bout a new breed, a new breed.

(repeat Verse)

CHORUS
A♭13   G♭13   F7(♯5♯9)   B♭7(♯5♯9)   A7(♯5♯9)
Armed and dangerous, strong and serious, clothed in righteousness. It's a new breed, a new breed.
A♭13   G♭13   F7(♯5♯9)   B♭7(♯5♯9)
Armed and dangerous, strong and serious, clothed in righteousness. It's a new breed, a new breed.

(repeat Verse)

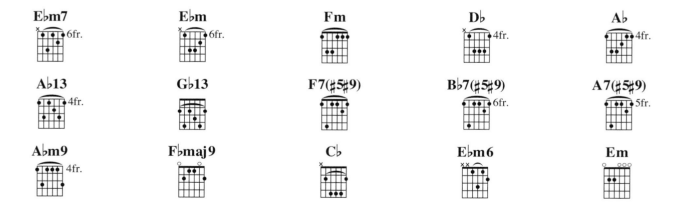

E♭m7   E♭m   Fm   D♭   A♭

A♭13   G♭13   F7(♯5♯9)   B♭7(♯5♯9)   A7(♯5♯9)

A♭m9   F♭maj9   C♭   E♭m6   Em

I Hear The Sound (page 2 of 2)

INSTRUMENTAL
E♭m Fm/E♭ E♭m *(repeat)*

BRIDGE 1

        E♭m7   **A♭m9**   **E♭m/G♭ Fm/A♭**

It ain't a black thing. It ain't a white thing. It ain't a colored thing. It's a kingdom thing.

E♭m7 A♭m9 E♭m/G♭ Fm/A♭

(no vocals)

        E♭m7   **F♭maj9**   **E♭m/G♭ Fm/A♭**

It ain't a black thing. It ain't a white thing. It ain't a colored thing. It's a kingdom thing.
(repeat three times)

(repeat Chorus)

BRIDGE 2

N.C.

When we get to the gates, when we get to the gates, now, when we get to the gates, when we get to the gates,

                    E♭m   **C♭/E♭**   **E♭m6**

We're gonna start taking it back, taking it back, taking it back, taking it back,

Em

Taking it back, taking it back, taking it back, taking it back.

(repeat Bridge 2 several times)
(repeat Chorus)

So Easy To Love/Friend Of God

Donald Clay

INTRO
  F#m7(4) E2/G# Amaj7 C#m7(4)

CHORUS
        F#m7(4) E2/G#   A2   C#m7(4)
It's so easy to love You. It's so easy to love You.
    F#m7(4)   B7sus   E   F#m7 E2/G#
It's so easy to love You,   because You're wonderful.
   Amaj7   E2/G#   C#m7
It's so easy to love You. It's so easy to love You.
   F#m7(4)   A2/B   A/E E D/F# E2/G#
It's so easy to love You,   because You're wonderful.
   Amaj9   E2/G#   C#m7(4)
It's so easy to love You. It's so easy to love You.
   F#m11   A2/B   E   F#m7 E2/G#
It's so easy to love You,   'cause You're wonderful.
   Amaj9   E2/G#   C#m7(4)
It's so easy to love You. It's so easy to love You.
   F#m11   A2/B   Esus4(2) E D/F# E2/G#
It's so easy to love You,   'cause You're mar-   velous.
   Amaj9   E2/G#   C#m7(4)
It's so easy to love You. It's so easy to love You.
   F#m11   A2/B   Dmaj7/E E7
It's so easy to love You,   'cause You're mar-   velous.
   Amaj9   E2/G#   C#m7(4)
It's so easy to love You. It's so easy to love You.
   F#m11   A2/B   Dmaj7/E E7
It's so easy to love You,   'cause You're glo-   rious.
   Amaj9   E2/G#   G#7(#5) C#m9 C#7(♭9)
It's so easy to love You. It's so easy to love You.
   F#m9   A2/B   E2 A2/E B/E A/E E2
It's so easy to love You,   You're my Friend.

FRIEND OF GOD *(Michael Grungor and Israel Houghton)*
CHORUS *(1st time Instrumental)*
  E   C#m7   F#m7(4)   E
I am a friend of God. I am a friend of God. I am a friend of God. He calls me friend.
(repeat and fade)

Friend Of God

Michael Gungor and Israel Houghton

CHORUS
 E   C#m7   F#m7(4)   E
 I am a friend of God, I am a friend of God, I am a friend of God, He calls me friend.

VERSE
 E   C#m7   F#m7(4)   E
 Who am I that You are mindful of me, that You hear me when I call?
 E   C#m7   F#m7(4)   D2
 Is it true that You are thinking of me? How You love me. It's amazing.

(repeat Verse)
(repeat Chorus twice)
(repeat Verse)

TRANSITION
   D D2   Dmaj7 F#m7 A2/B A D2
 It's amazing! It's amaz-   ing!

(repeat Chorus twice)

TRANSITION
   E2   F#m7(4)   E/A
 Yeah, yeah, yeah. He calls me friend, yeah, yeah, hoo.

BRIDGE
 E/A   E2/G#   F#m7(4)   A2
 God Almighty, Lord of Glory, You have called me friend.
 (repeat five times)

(repeat Chorus several times; optional drums only 3rd time, Instrumental 5th time; substitute lyrics "You call me friend.")

TAG
    E/G# E2/G#   F#m7(4)   E
 You call me friend.   You call me friend.   You call me friend.

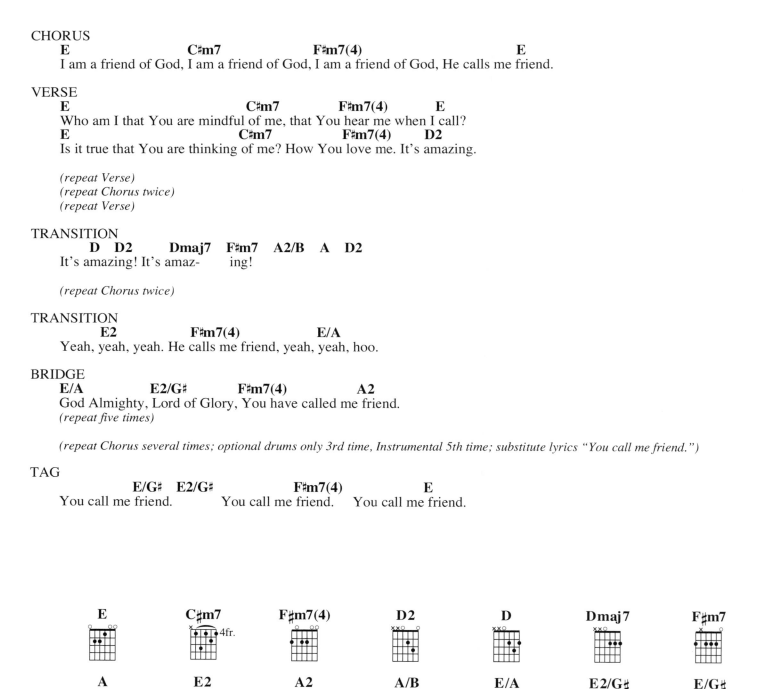

Friend

Israel Houghton, Meleasa Houghton, Aaron Lindsey and Kevin Singleton

INTRO
    A2/B

CHORUS
    E2   **E/G♯** **A2**   **B/D♯** **C♯m7**
    Friend, there will never be   a friend as dear to me as You.
                    Esus/B **E/B** **A2**   **A2/B**
    There will never   be   another closer than a brother.
    E2   **F♯m7**   **B7/F♯** **E2/G♯** **E/G♯** **E/A**   **B**   **C♯m9** **A/B**   **E** **Emaj7** **A/E**
    Friend, al-   ways   worth   the   wait, as faithful as the day; You say we are friends.
    (repeat)

VERSE
    E   **Emaj7** **A/E**   **E/G♯**   **A2**   **B7sus**   **E2**
    Woh, woh,   woh. You know all about me, the good and the bad.
     E/G♯   **E/A** **B7sus** **E** **F♯m7** **E/G♯**   **A2**   **B7sus**   **C♯m9**
    You know when I rise   and   fall.   You see my beginning, You stand at the end.
    Cmaj7   **D**   **Am9**   **Bm7**
    And yet, You remain faithful to say I'm Your friend.

    (repeat Chorus)
    (repeat Verse and Chorus)

BRIDGE
    E   **B/D♯**   **E/D**   **A2/C♯** **Am9**   **Bm7**   **E**
    Every time You call me, I receive Your healing; Every time You call me friend.
    (repeat four times)
    E   **B/D♯**   **E/D**   **A2/C♯** **Am9**   **Bm7** **C**   **D** **C/E**   **D/F♯** **E**
    Every time You call me, I receive Your healing; Every time You call,   every time You call, every time You call me friend.

    (repeat Chorus)

TAG
    Bsus **E/B** **B** **A/B**   **Bsus** **E/B** **B** **A/B**   **Bsus** **E/B** **B** **A/B**   **Amaj7/B** **B7**   **B7sus**
    You say,   You say,   You say,   You say   we are friends.

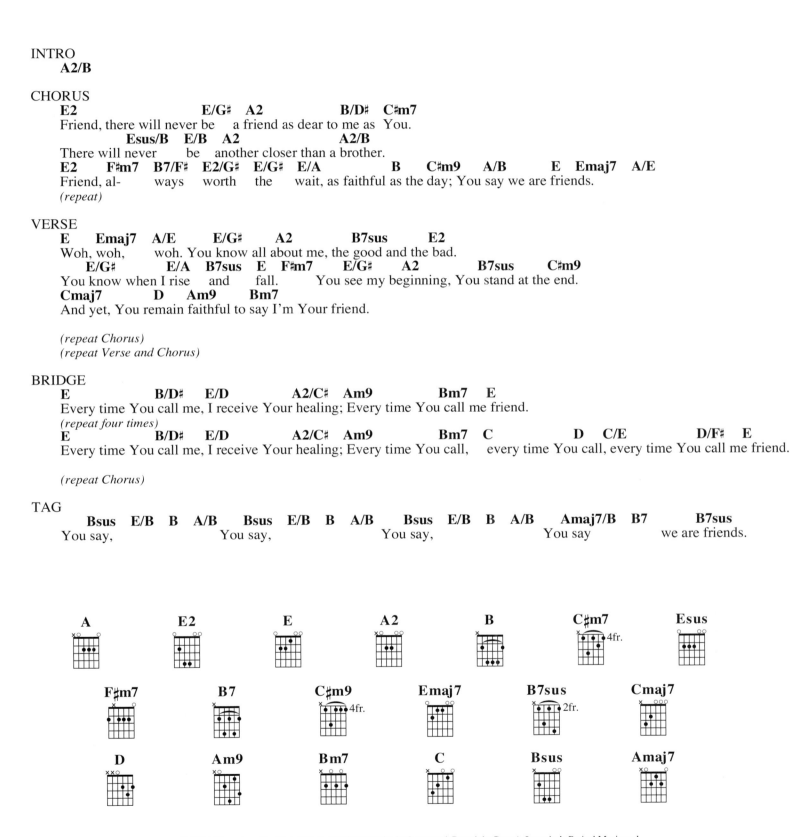

Friend Medley (page 1 of 2)

JOY OF MY DESIRE *(Jennifer Randolph)*

E2 E/A E2/G# F#m9 Bm7 E13   Amaj7 E2/G# C#m11 F#m7 Bm7(4) E7
There will never be a friend as dear to me,   there will never be a friend   as dear to me,

    Amaj9 B/C# F#m7 B7sus E2 Bm9 E F#m7
There will never be a friend as dear to me as You, You.

  E2/G# A B/A E/G# Esus/F# E Bm7(4) E E/G#
I worship You. I worship You in spir- it and in truth.

A D/A A B/A Amaj7 G#m F#m7(4) B/E F#m2/D# D7(b5b9) D7(b9) C#m7 F#7
I worship You   in spirit and in truth.

   F#m11 E2/G# A B/C# E#dim7   F#m11 E2/G# A Amaj7 C/D
There will never be a friend as dear to me,   there will never be a friend as dear to me.

Bb/C F/Bb Gm/Bb F/Bb F2/A C/D Dm7 Gm7 F/A Dm/B Dm/C C
There will nev- er be a friend as dear to me as ...

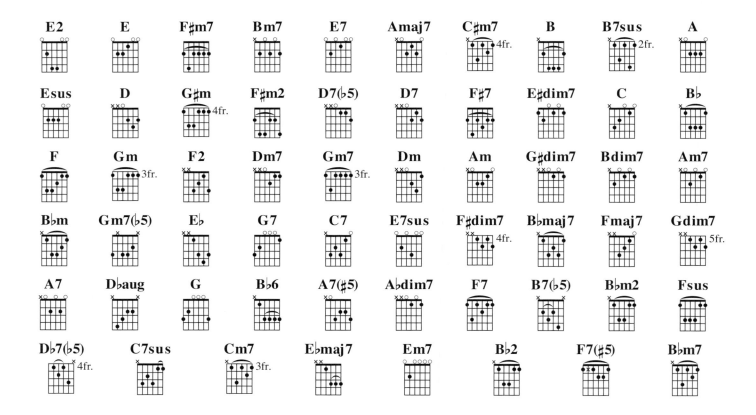

Friend Medley (page 2 of 2)

NO, NOT ONE *(Johnson Oatman, Jr. and George C. Hugg)*

```
     F         Am/C    F   Gm    G#dim  F/A   Bdim7   Bb   Bdim7         F2/A   Am7   Dm7   Bbm/G
There's, there's not a   friend              like the  lowly      Jesus–
F/C            Dm     Gm7(b5)  F  Eb  Dm  G13  Bb/C  C          F   Bb/F  F
No, no, no, no, no, not   one,                        no, not one!
Bb/C  F2     Am/C   C13   F   Gm   G#dim7  F/A   Bdim7   Bb   E7sus/B  E7   Am7   Dm7   Gm7(b5)
There's, there's not an   hour              that He is,       He's     not   near us–
      F2/C    F#dim7  Gm   F   Eb  Dm  G13        Bbmaj7/C  C       Fmaj7  Bb/F  Bb/C
Woh no, no, not one!                  Woh no,         no, not one!
C   Bb/C  C   F2   Bb/F  F2/A   Bbm   F/A   Gdim   F   G13   Gm/C   F
For        Jesus knows,  He knows   all    about our    trou-  ble,
D7(#9)  A7    Dm   Dbaug     F/C   Bbm6   F/A   G13   G/B        Bb6/C   A7(#5)
And     He will     guide        till the day,     the day is done;
A7      F/A   Abdim7   Gm7        F7
There's not a friend,         there's not a friend,
      B7(b5)        Bb        Bdim7   F2/C   Gm7(b5)   F/A   Bbm2   F2/C
There's not a friend like the low, the lowly     Jesus.
     Bbm6   Bbm/G  F7/A   Bbm   F/C   C/D   Dm7   Gm7(b5)   F/A   Bbm6   F/C
No, not one.                    No,   not   one.
C/D   Dm7   Bbm6   Bbm/G   F7/A   Bbm   F/A   Am/D   Dm7   Gm7(b5)   G13   Bbmaj7/C   C
No,   not   one.                     No,   not   one,   no,   not,   not one.
```

WHAT A FRIEND WE HAVE IN JESUS *(Joseph M. Scriven and Charles C. Converse)*

```
   B    C    Dm7   C7/E   F   Fsus/G   F/A   F7
O what peace we    often  for,      forfeit,
Bb   F2/A   Dm7   Db7(b5)   C9sus
O what needless pain we bear,        we bear,
F    Cm9    F7    Bb
All because we do not carry,
          Bdim7   F/C   Dm7   G13   Bb/C   C   F   Bb/C
All we gotta do is carry       every- thing to God   in  prayer.
     C      F2    Ebmaj7/F   F7   F/A   Bb   Bdim7
What a Friend, say. What a Friend  we have in   Je-  sus,
F/C   Dm7   G13        C9sus   C/D   Db9
All       our sins and griefs to bear!
Cm9   Eb/F   F/A   Bb   Bdim7   F/C   Dm7(4)   G/B   Bbm6   Dm   F/C   G/B   Bbm6
What a privi- lege to car- ry     every-        thing to God in  prayer,
F2/A   Dm7(4)   Em11   A7(#5)   A7   Dm   F/C   G/B   Bbm6
Every-          thing to God     in   prayer,
F2/A   Dm7   G13   Bbmaj7/C   C7(b9)   F2
Every-      thing to God     in       prayer.
```

FRIEND *(Israel Houghton, Meleasa Houghton, Aaron Lindsey and Kevin Singleton)*

```
              C/F   F/Eb            Bb2/D   F7(#5)   Bbm9   Cm7          F2
And every time You call me,    I receive Your healing.    O every time    You call me friend.
```

Rise Within Us *with* **Another Breakthrough** (page 1 of 2)

Israel Houghton and Aaron Lindsey

INTRO
Fm9   Eb2/G   Abmaj7   Bb   C(no3)

                                  Cm9   **Bb/C**
Rise within us, Holy Spirit.   Rise with healing,   healing in Your wings.
C   **Fm9**   **Eb2/G**   **Abmaj7** **Bb** **Csus**
Rise within us, Holy Spirit.   We're ready,   ready,   ready   for You.

VERSE 1
Dm11   **C/E** **Fmaj9**   **G7** **Am7** **Fm9**   **Eb2/G**   **Abmaj7**   **Bb** **Csus** **C**
    Rise within us,   Holy Spirit.   We're ready, we're ready, we're ready for   You.
(repeat twice)

VERSE 2
Dm11 (Ebm11-*on repeat*) **Db/F** **Gbmaj7**   **Ab7** **Bbm7** **Gbm9**   **Fb2/Ab**   **Bbbmaj7**   **Cb** **Dbsus** **Db**
    Rise with power,   Holy Spirit.   We're calling, we're calling, we're calling on   You.
(repeat)

VERSE 3
Ebm11   **Db/F** **Gbmaj7**   **Ab7** **Bbm7** **Gbm9**   **Fb2/Ab**   **Amaj7**   **Cb** **Dbsus** **Db**
    Rise with healing,   Holy Spirit.   We're desperate, we're desperate, we're desperate for   You.
(repeat)

VERSE 4
Ebm11 (Em11-*on repeat*) **D/F#** **Gmaj7**   **A7** **Bm7** **Gm9**   **F2/A**   **Bbmaj7**   **C** **Dsus** **D**
    Show Your glory,   Holy Spirit.   We're longing, we're longing, we're longing for   You.
(repeat)

Rise Within Us *with* **Another Breakthrough (page 2 of 2)**

INSTRUMENTAL
B♭maj9/C   Amaj9/B   A♭maj9/B♭   Gmaj9/A   G♯7(♯5♯9)

F♯7(♯5♯9)   D♯dim7   Gm9   F2/A   B♭maj7   C   Dsus   D

VERSE 5 *(1st time Instrumental)*
Bm7/E   D/F♯ Gmaj7   A7   Bm7   Gm9   F2/A   B♭maj7   C   Dsus   D
    Rise with healing,   Holy Spirit.   We're desperate, we're desperate, we're desperate for   You.
(repeat)

TRANSITION
Em11   F♯m7   Gmaj7   A   Bm7   Gm9

ANOTHER BREAKTHROUGH *(Israel Houghton and Aaron Lindsey)*
   Am7   B♭maj7   C   B♭maj7   C   B♭maj7   G/C
We're ready, we're ready, we're ready for a break-   through, break-   through,
       F2/B♭   C   Cm7   B♭2/D   E♭2   F   Gm7
Hoo, for a break-   through, break-   through.

Another Breakthrough

Israel Houghton and Aaron Lindsey

INTRO
Cm7(4)   B♭2/D   E♭2   F2   Gm7

VERSE 1
Cm7(4)   B♭/D   E♭2   F   Gm7   Cm7(4)   B♭/D   E♭maj7   D/F♯   Gm7
   Another level,   another harvest,   another day for You to manifest Your promises.
Cm7(4)   B♭2/D   E♭2   F   Gm7   G♭maj7   A♭   B♭sus   B♭   Dm7   Gm7
   Another moment,   another season for a   break- through, break- through.
(repeat twice)

TRANSITION
F♯m7   G♯m7

VERSE 2
C♯m7(4)   B2/D♯   E2   F♯   G♯m7   C♯m7(4)   B2/D♯   C♯2/E♯   D♯/G   G♯m7(4)
   A greater level,   a greater harvest,   a greater day for You to manifest Your promises.
C♯m7(4)   B2/D♯   E2   F♯   G♯m7   Gmaj7   A   C♯m/B   B
   A greater moment,   a greater season for a   break- through, break- through.
(repeat)

TRANSITION
Em7   Am7(4)

VERSE 3
Dm7(4)   C2/E   F2   G   Am7   Dm7(4)   C2/E   D2/F♯   E/G♯   Am7(4)
   This is the level,   this is my harvest,   this is the day for You to manifest Your promises.
Dm7(4)   C2/E   Fmaj9   G   Am7   A♭maj7   B♭   Dm/C   C   Em7   Am7
   This is my moment,   this is my season for a   break- through, break- through.
(repeat)

BRIDGE
A♭maj7   B♭   B♭/D   C/E   Fm9   Gm7   Dm/C   C
Break-   through, break- through, break- through, break- through.
(repeat as desired - optional Instrumental on some repeats)

INSTRUMENTAL TAG
C   Csus   C   B♭/C   B♭sus/C   B♭/C   A♭/C   B♭2/C
(repeat as desired)

Cm7(4)   B♭2   E♭2   F2   Gm7   B♭   F   E♭maj7   D   G♭maj7

A♭   B♭sus   Dm7   F♯m7   A♭m7(G♯m7)   C♯m7(4)   B2   E2   F♯   C♯2

D♯   G♯m7(4)   Gmaj7   A   C♯m   B   Em7   Am7(4)   Dm7(4)   C2

G   Am7   D2   E   Fmaj9   A♭maj7   Dm   C   Fm9   Csus

Lord Of The Breakthrough

Israel Houghton and Aaron Lindsey

INTRO
C2 B♭/C Fm/A♭ B♭2 *(repeat as desired)*
C F/C C B♭/C B♭sus/C B♭/C A♭maj7 B♭ B♭2

CHORUS
C   Csus C   B♭/C   B♭sus/C B♭/C
Lord of the break- through,   Lord of the break-   through,
A♭maj7   B♭
You are the Lord of the breakthrough, and we worship You, we worship You.

(repeat as desired, with optional Instrumental/Vocal ad lib on repeat)

INSTRUMENTAL
C2 Csus

BRIDGE *(Vocal ad lib section)*
G/A   Am7 Dm7(4)
I stand in awe of You tonight, O God.   Every promise that You've said... *(repeat as desired)*
Am9 Dm7 C/D   Am7   Dm11   Am9   B♭2   Am7
I see the Lord,   I see the Lord   exalted high upon the worship of the people of the earth.
Dm9   G/A   Dm11   G/A
I see the Lord, I see the Lord, and I'll never be the same, You take my breath away, O Lord.

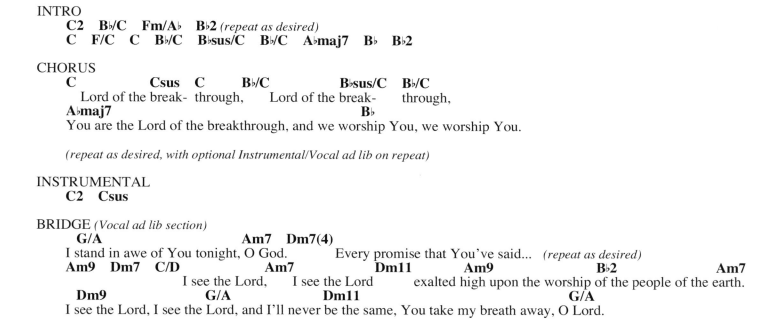

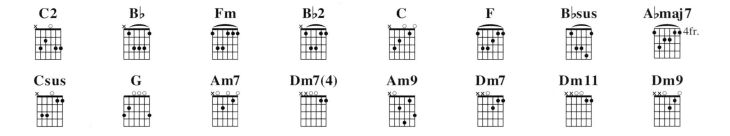

Breathe Into Me

Israel Houghton

VERSE
 Am7(4) **Dm7(4)** **G/A** **Am7(4)** **Dm7(4)** **G/A**
   Only You take my breath away. Only You take my breath away.
 Am7(4) **Dm7(4)**   **Em7** **Am7**   **Dm**   **C/E** **D/F♯** **Asus**
 Only You take my breath away. Then You breathe new life into me.

VERSE *(in D)*
 A **Em7(4)**   **Bm7(4)**   **Em7(4)**   **Bm7(4)**
 Only You take my breath away. Nobody else but You take my breath   away.
   Em7(4)   **F♯m7** **Bm7**   **Em**   **D/F♯** **E/G♯** **C**
 Only You, Jesus, take my breath away. Then You breathe new life into me.

CHORUS
 Gmaj7   **Bm11** **Gmaj7**
 So breathe into me,   just breathe into me,
Bm11 **C♯m9** **Gmaj7**   **Gmaj9/A**
 Oh,   just breathe into me, Oh Lord, once again.

(repeat Verse twice)

EXTENDED CHORUS
 Gmaj7   **Bm11** **Gmaj7**   **Bm11** **C♯m9**
 So breathe into me,   just breathe into me,
  Gmaj7   **Gmaj7/A** **G/A** **A** **D** **Em7** **D/F♯** **E2/G♯**
 Lord, breathe into me,   once again.
(repeat)

FINAL CHORUS
 Gmaj7   **Bm11** **Gmaj7**   **Bm11** **C♯m9**
 So breathe into me,   just breathe into me,
  Gmaj7   **G/A**   **Bm**
 Lord, breathe into me, once again.

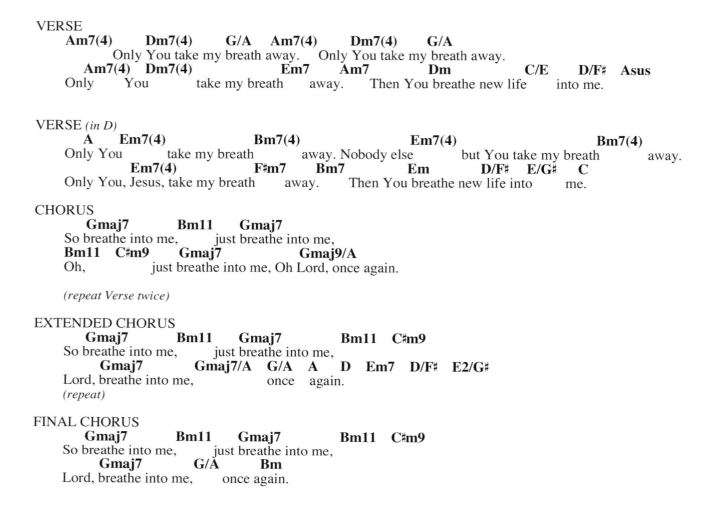

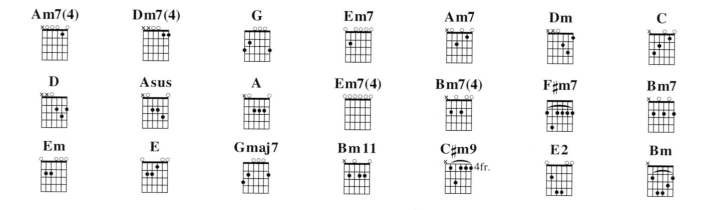

Awesome Medley: I Stand In Awe (Maravillado Estoy)
Mark Altrogge

INTRO
Bm   F#/A#   Bm   A/C#   D   Em7   D2/F#   D/F#   B7(♭9)
B/D#   Em   B/D#   Em   D/F#   G   A   Dsus   D
F#2/A#   Bm   F#/A#   Bm   A/C#   D   F#dim   Em7
B/D#   Em   D/F#   G   E/G#   Asus   A
F#/A#   Bm   F#/A#   B/A   F#m7   B   Gmaj9   Em/G   Gmaj7   Em7(4)   Asus   A

VERSE

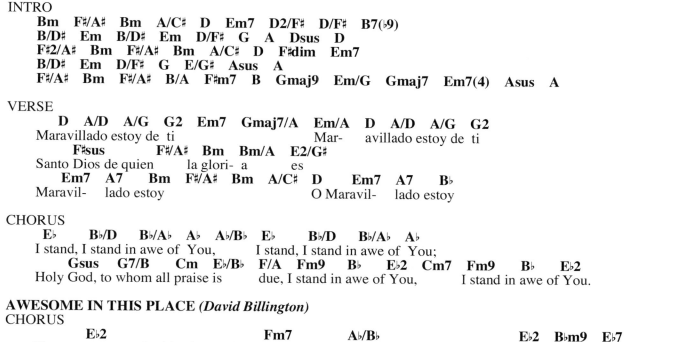

CHORUS

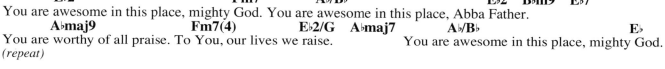

AWESOME IN THIS PLACE *(David Billington)*
CHORUS

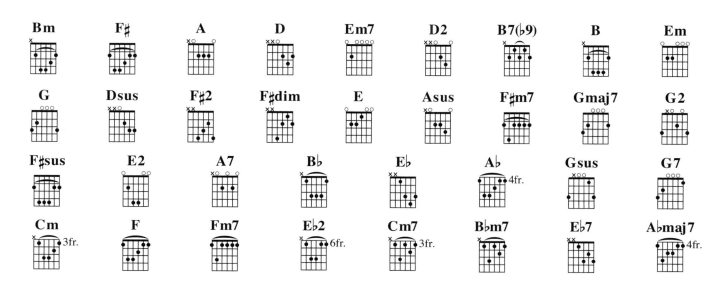

Here I Am To Worship *with* You Are Good

Tim Hughes

INTRO
    E   B/E   D/E   A/E *(repeat several times)*

VERSE 1
    E   B/E   D/E   A/E   E   B/E   D/E A/E
    Light of the world, You stepped down into darkness; Opened my eyes, let me see.
    E   B/E   D/E A/E   E   B/E   A2
    Beauty that made this heart adore You, hope of a life spent with You.

CHORUS
    F♯m/A E/A F♯m/A E   B/D♯   E/G♯   A2
    Here   I am to   worship, here I am to bow down, here I am to say that You're my God.
                     E   B/D♯   E/G♯   A2 B/A A/B
    You're altogether lovely, altogether worthy, altogether wonderful to me.

VERSE 2
    E   B/E   D/E   A/E E   B/E   D/E A/E
    King of all days, O so highly exalted, glorious in heaven above.
    E   B/E   D/E   A/E E   B/E   A2
    Humbly You came to the earth You created,   all for love's sake became poor.

(repeat Chorus)

BRIDGE
     B   E/G♯   A2   B   E/G♯ A2
    I'll never know how much it cost to see my sin upon that cross.
    (repeat 3 times)
    (repeat Chorus as desired)

YOU ARE GOOD *(Israel Houghton)*
    F♯m/A E/A F♯m/A E   B/E D/E A/E E   B/E   D/E A/E
    Here   I am to   worship You. Hallelujah! I worship You for who You are.
    E   B/E D/E A/E E2/G♯ Bm9   C D/C
    I worship You. Hallelujah! I worship You for who You are,
         C D/C   C D/C   C D/C   C D/C   D
    Who You are,   who You are,   who You are,   who You are,   who You are.

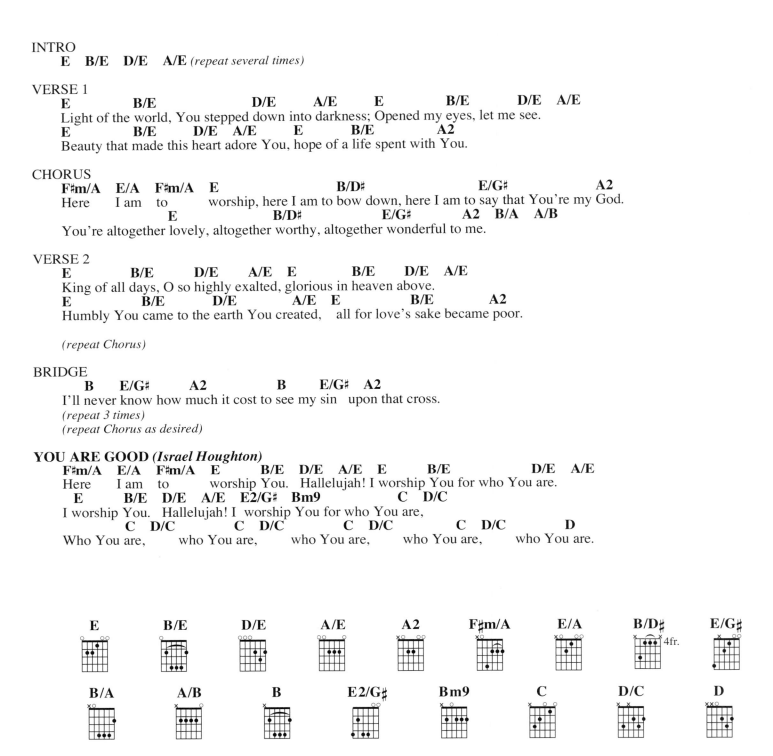

Holy

Israel Houghton, Meleasa Houghton and Aaron Lindsey

CHORUS
D   E2   B2
Magnificent and ho-holy,
F#m7 E/G# A2 Amaj7/B E2 B2   F#m7 E/G# A2 B7sus
Ho- ho-   ly,   holy, You are holy.

VERSE 1
E2 B2 F#m7 E/G# A2 B7sus B Bsus B
Ho-holy, ho- ho- ly,
E2 E F#m E/G# C#m/A# B2 F#m7 E/G# A2 Bb/C
Ho-   ho-   ly, ho- ho- ly.

VERSE 1 *(in F)*
F Dm/F C2 Gm7 F/A Bb2 Bb/C
Ho-ho-   ly, ho- ho- ly.
F Dm/F C2 Gm7 F/A Bb2 Db7sus
Ho-ho-   ly, ho- ho- ly.

VERSE 2 *(in Gb)*
Gb Ebm/Gb Db2 Db Gdim7 Abm7 Gb/Bb C2 Cb/Db
Wor-   thy,   wor-   thy!
Gb Ebm/Gb Db2 Db Gdim7 Abm7 Gb/Bb C2 D7sus
Wor-   thy,   wor-   thy!

VERSE 3 *(in G)*
G Em/G D G#dim7 Am G/B C2 C/D
Might-   y,   might-   y!
G Em/G D G#dim7 Am G/B C2 C/D
Might-   y,   might-   y!

INSTRUMENTAL
G/D Em/D D Am/D G/D C2/D D C/D
G/D Em/D D G#dim7 Am G/B C2 C/D D C/D D

VERSE 4
G Em/G D G#dim7 Am G/B C2 C/D D C/D D
Ho- ho-   ly,   ho- ho- ly.
G Em/G D G#dim7 Am G/B C2
Ho- ho-   ly,   ho- ho- ly.

Chord diagrams: D, E2, B2 (Cb2), F#m7, E, A2, Amaj7, B7sus (2fr.), B (Cb), Bsus, F#m, C#m (4fr.), Bb, F, Dm, C2, Gm7 (3fr.), Bb2, Db7sus (4fr.), Gb, Ebm, Db2 (4fr.), Db (4fr.), Gdim7 (5fr.), Abm7 (4fr.), D7sus, G, Em, G#dim7, Am, C

Going To Another Level (page 1 of 2)

Israel Houghton and Aaron Lindsey

INTRO
G(no3)   F/G   C/G   G(no3)   F/G   C/G
Woh,   woh.
(repeat several times)

CHORUS
G(no3)   Fmaj9/G   G(no3)
I'm goin' to another level. I said, I'm   goin' to another level.
         F/G   C/G   G(no3)   F/G   C/G   G(no3)   G13   G♭13   G13
Everybody, help me say!   I'm goin' to another level.   I'm goin' to another level.

CHORUS *(in A♭)*
G♭maj9/A♭   G♭/A♭   D♭/A♭   A♭(no3)   E♭m/G♭   D♭/F
I'm goin' to another level.   I'm goin' to another level.
A♭13   E♭m/G♭   D♭/F
    Don't stop reachin', keep believin'. Come on, we're goin' to another level.
A♭13   A♭13   G13   A♭13
    Don't stop pressin' for your blessin'. Come on, we're goin' to another level.   Yeah!

CHORUS *(in A)*
Gmaj9/A   G/A   D/A   A(no3)   Em/G   D/F♯
I'm goin' to another level.   I'm goin' to another level.
A13   Em/G   D/F♯
    Don't stop reachin', keep believin'. Come on, goin' to another level.
A13   A13   A♭13   A13
    Don't stop pressin' for your blessin'. Come on, goin' to another level.

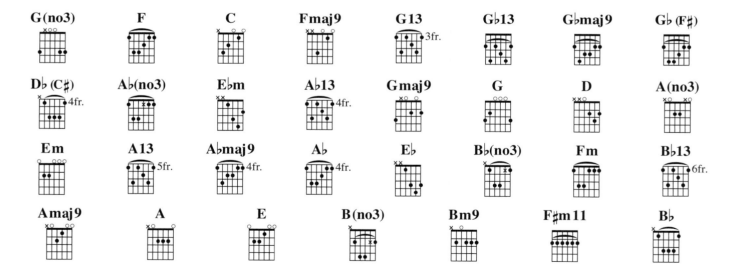

Going To Another Level (page 2 of 2)

CHORUS *(in B♭)*

A♭maj9/B♭   **A♭/B♭**   **E♭/B♭**   **B♭(no3)**   **Fm/A♭**

I'm goin' to another level.   I'm goin' to another level.

BRIDGE

E♭/G   **A♭/B♭**   **E♭/B♭**   **B♭(no3)**   **A♭/B♭**   **E♭/B♭**   **B♭(no3)**

Woh,   woh,   woh! *(repeat several times)*

B♭13   **A♭13**   **B♭13**

You gotta keep pressin' on, gotta keep on pressin' on! *(repeat several times)*

CHORUS *(in B)*

Amaj9/B   **A/B**   **E/B**   **B(no3)**   **A/B**   **E/B**

I'm goin' to another level.   I'm goin' to another level.

BRIDGE *(in B - first several times Instrumental)*

Bm9   **F♯m11**   **Gmaj9/B**   **F♯m11**

Gotta keep pressin' on, gotta keep on   pressin' on!

(repeat as desired)

TAG

N.C.   **D/C**   **E/D**   **F♯/E**   **G/F♯**   **B♭/F♯**   **C♯/F♯**   **E/F♯**   **G/F♯**   **B(no3)**

I'm goin' to another level.